COMPLETE BARBELL OUTFIT

$5.00

NOW, LOWEST PRICE EVER OFFERED

TRILENE
RECD
TABLETS
CURE
for
STOUTNESS
Registered
by
GOVERNMENT
Price 2/6

FOR
YOUR
THROAT

Are you
unlucky?
Now you can
do something
about it

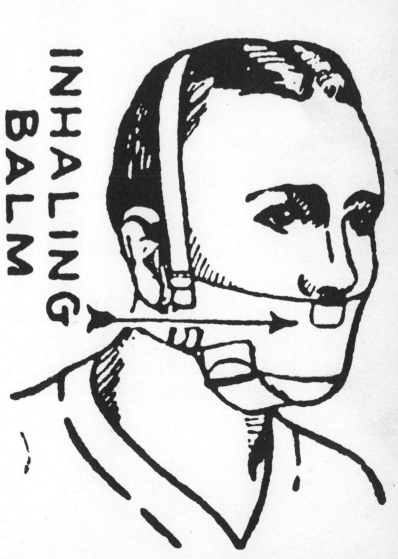

INHALING
BALM

To Paul –
Christmas 1980
With much love & best wishes
from – Mum and Philip

Published by The Hamlyn Publishing Group Limited
London · New York · Sydney · Toronto
Astronaut House, Feltham, Middlesex, England.

Copyright © The Hamlyn Publishing Group Limited,
1979.
ISBN 0 600 366 030

Printed in Italy

The World of
SMALL ADS

"You've been a better Club Secretary since we bought you a typewriter, Jim"

Everybody needs a Remington Portable these days—secretaries, business men, authors, doctors, lawyers, teachers, students—and the family at home! Invaluable for correspondence, notes, lectures, literary work, etc. Very simple in construction and delightfully easy to use. Weight only 11 lb.—size $12\frac{1}{2}" \times 12" \times 5"$ complete with handsome carrying-case. For full particulars, send coupon to-day—or apply to your local Dealer or Stationer.

REMINGTON

HOME PORTABLE

Assembled in Great Britain by British Labour
£9 : 9 : 0 cash

The World of
SMALL ADS

Mario Lippa & David Newton

**A fascinating look at the world
of advertising mini art**

HAMLYN · LONDON · NEW YORK · SYDNEY · TORONTO

"You too can have a body like mine"

THE BODY — PAGES 13-64

"They laughed when I sat down to play the piano"

SELF IMPROVEMENT — PAGES 65-74

"A hard man is good to find"

SEX — PAGES 75-86

Acknowledgements

The authors wish to thank the many advertisers who gave their kind permission to reproduce examples of the advertisements shown in this book. It has proved impossible to trace the copyright holders of certain advertisements. We apologise for credits omitted and would be happy to rectify the matter in future editions should the necessary information come to light.

Thanks are also due to our researcher Diana Greene, photographer Peter Davis and to the private collections of various individuals. Material was also supplied by the Western Americana Picture Library, The Mansell Collection and The Zenka Woodward Picture Library. For the preparation of camera ready artwork our special thanks to Long John's Workshop.

"Thank goodness, Hotpoint are going to make life easier after the war!"

THE WAR YEARS 1914-18 1939-45 — PAGES 87-94

"You've been a better club secretary since we bought you a typewriter, Jim."

WORK AND PLAY — PAGES 95-112

"Create a neighbourhood sensation..."

MISCELLANEOUS — PAGES 113-124

Introduction

The buying and selling of slaves and property and the coming and going of merchant ships were the subject of some of the earliest examples of small ads. and as such, represented some of the activities of the early American settlers.

50 DOLLARS REWARD.—Ran away, on the 21st of July, from the subscriber, living near Chaptico, St. Mary's county, Md., negro WILLIAM. His wearing apparel cannot be accurately described, as he took with him a variety. William is about five feet six inches high, and well built, and so bright a mulatto that at first sight he would be taken for a white man. His hair is brown, and nearly straight; he has a wide mouth, and a very fine set of teeth. His voice is coarse, and when spoken to his eyes, though generally turned towards the ground, are rolled suddenly upwards, so as to display the balls considerably. William, having left home without cause, is doubtless making his way to a free State.

I will give the above reward to any person who will bring him home, or secure him in jail so that I get him again.
THOMAS W. GARDINER,
july 28—w2m   Near Chaptico, St. Mary's co. Md.

To a collector of Americana it seems that these items give a rare insight into a familiar phase of history. To many people, slavery who have read very ma

By 1880 advertising was becoming commonplace across the USA and gaining ground rapidly in the UK, blossoming at the onset of the Industrial Revolution.

Much can be learned from the small ads. about late Victorian life in England that the history books won't tell you.

An avalanche of inventions and gadgets poured onto the market. Many failed because they were basically impractical but others succeeded and became the forerunners of many household appliances that we now consider necessities.

Of course, gadgetry was not the only thing sold off the page. Those esoteric products offering a more personal benefit existed in abundance.

Products to shrink your hemorrhoids, keep your teeth radiant white, cover up ugly veins, erase acne, pimples, blackheads and oily skin. Products to remove unwanted hair, grow hair where it wouldn't grow before, ease ruptures, give you power over others and promise you eternal youth crammed the columns of newspapers and magazines at the time and believe it or not, still do.

Little has changed in the basic sales pitch over the last 100 years.

The compelling combination of words and pictures is still evident and all the more important when operating on a small scale.

Charles Roman, an advertising executive is credited with composing the first Charles Atlas ads. in the 1920's.

Copy lines like 'The insult that made a man out of Mack' and 'Quit kicking sand in our faces' have now been absorbed into the language.

That the 'pen is mightier than the sword' is a credo that may well hold a lot of truth when it comes to examining the small ad.

Yet the graphics themselves also bear considerable study. Their economy of statement and ability to communicate can be formidable. The imagery used in 'Release the slender you inside,' for example, says it all.

The direct simplicity of the artwork used for , 'Invisible Liftee height pads,' communicates brilliantly in the small ad. format and the 'before and after' visual is still a tried and trusted technique.

In the beauty stakes the bosom has always had its fair share of exposure. Reflect for a moment on some of the claims. 'A lovely bosom is a woman's rightful possession.' 'Bust beauty with amazing BUTIFORM Oral cosmetic' and another, for those who believe that the body is the true key to feminine allure; 'For bosom beauty try the one tested, trusted body cream that contains 40,000 units of Estrogenic Hormones.'

One product category that is now sold more openly, over the counter so to speak, is sex.

From the famous Chicken Ranch brothel outside Las Vegas, 'Easy turn round for trucks,' to the more tongue-in cheek massage parlours. 'Alice will take you into Wonderland,' promises one.

Other girls, Katrina, Natasha, Fleur, Lolita and Emmanuelle offer similar experiences including a 24 hour service, visiting facilities and a menu of treatments to match their exotic names.

A whole new field of 'hardware' has sprung up in the wake of the 'liberated' society of the 60's and 70's. A vast range of products from vibrators to lifesize blow—up sex dolls that are 'never satisfied.'

To us the world of small ads. resembles a kind of two-dimensional streetmarket. A rough tough environment where getting noticed means the difference between 'sale' and 'no sale.' An enviroment in which success comes to those who offer to fulfill a need and present it with flair and imagination. Many of the words and graphics are of intrinsic interest in themselves, and reflect not only the development of promotional techniques but also an intriguing image of our society, its interests, obsessions and priorities.

"You too can have a body like mine"

Probably one of the most famous copy lines of our time. A healthy muscular body is obviously a product that, for some, answers a long felt want. Tripping over the heels of Charles Atlas, similar products came thick and fast. 'Add 3 inches of steel-like muscles to your arms.' 'The strongest arms in the world.' 'For power-packed inches to your chest fast.' The composers of these ads. have flexed their visual and verbal muscles and the results are often very impressive.

For the less fortunate of us it would seem that the body is in a constant state of collapse. From the top of the head to the soles of the feet there is a product to suit a particular ailment. And what is more, the need for many of them does not seem to pass with time.

Head gear

Hand Grip

for weight lifting

Giant cable pull

Rowing machine

foot gear

16

IMPOSSIBLE?

NOT FOR THE SUPER BODYBUILDING SYSTEM!

BE BETTER THAN THE BEST, BE DYNAMIC!

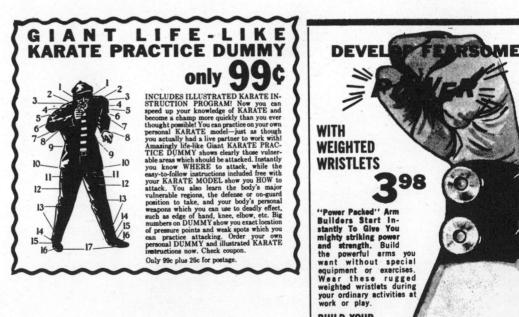

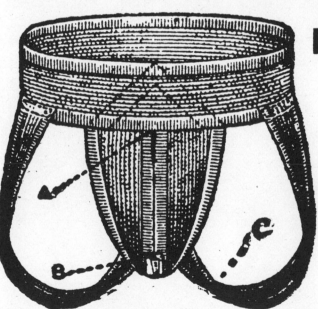

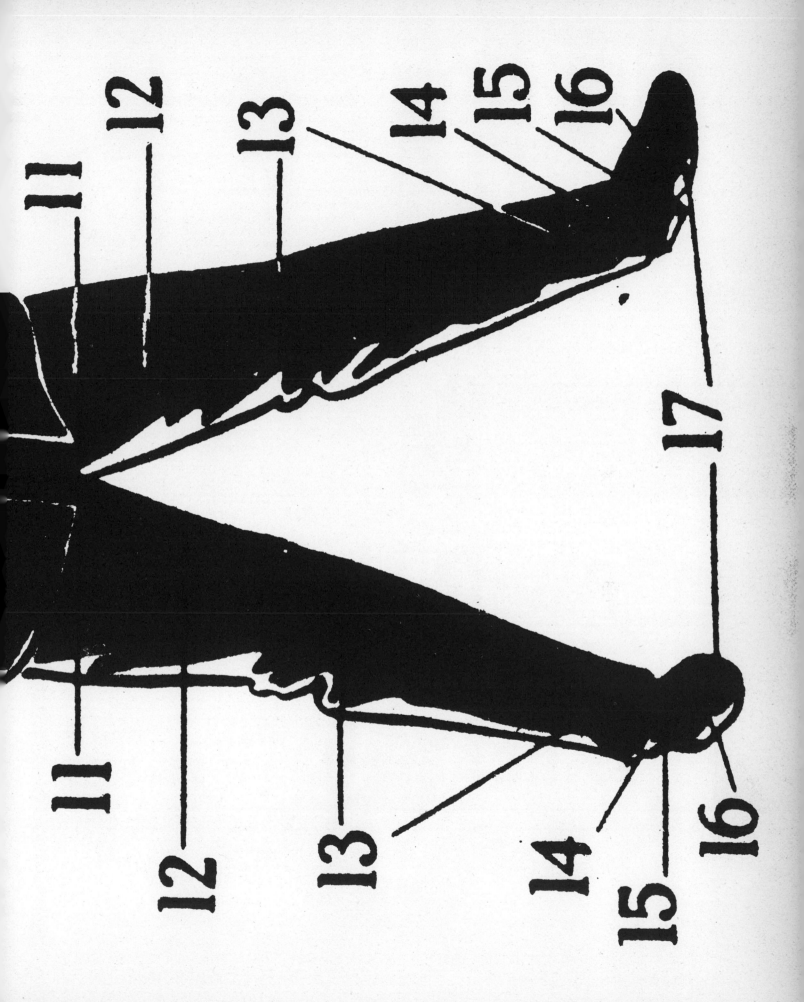

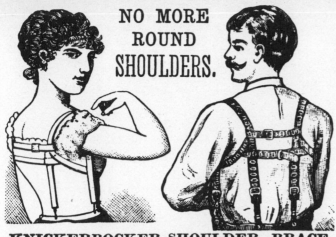

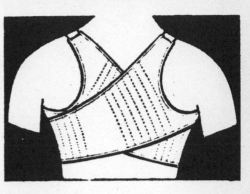
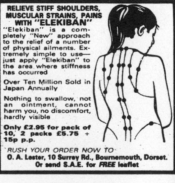

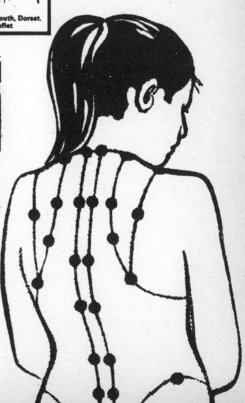

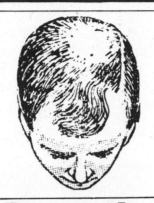
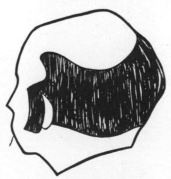
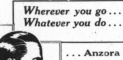

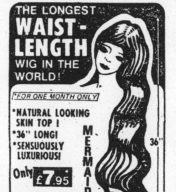

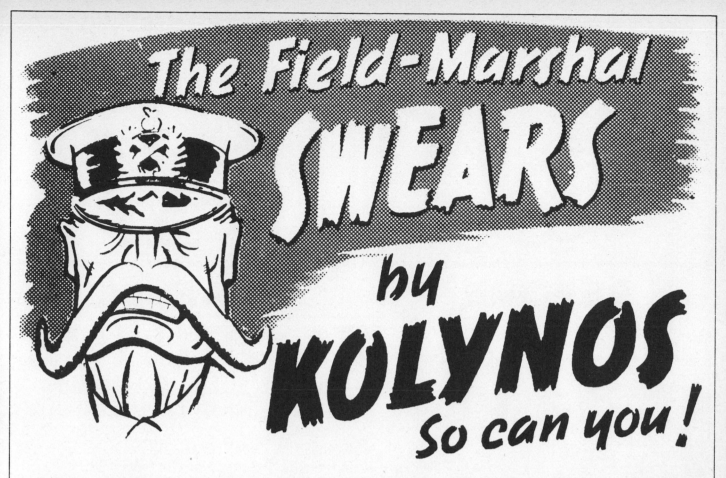

27

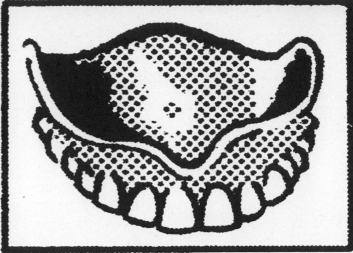

BEFORE

AFTER

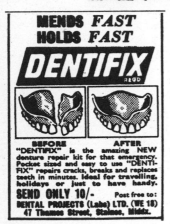

Let's look up and Smile . . .

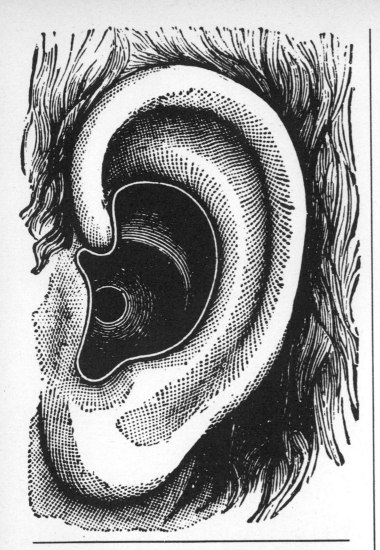

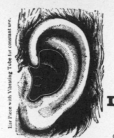
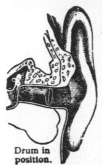

THE ELECTRICPATENT SOCKS.

FOR CREATING A CONSTANT ELECTRIC CURRENT AND PRODUCING A HIGH DEGREE OF WARMTH.

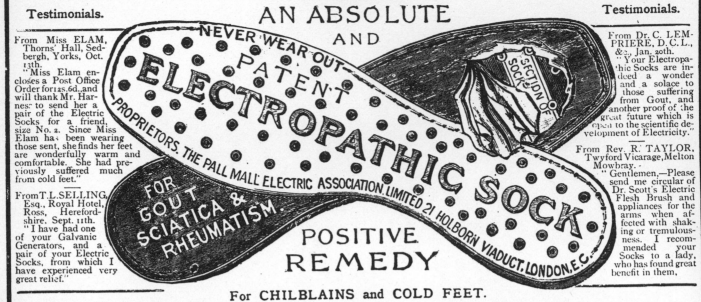

AN ABSOLUTE AND

NEVER WEAR OUT

PATENT

ELECTROPATHIC SOCK

PROPRIETORS, THE PALL MALL ELECTRIC ASSOCIATION, LIMITED 21 HOLBORN VIADUCT, LONDON, E.C.

FOR GOUT SCIATICA & RHEUMATISM.

POSITIVE REMEDY

SECTION OF SOCK

For CHILBLAINS and COLD FEET.

The SOCKS are simply put inside the shoes or boots, and after wearing them a short time a continued and most beneficial warmth penetrates the body.

These ELECTRIC SOCKS prove the best means for keeping the feet warm, for creating bodily comfort, and preventing illness; they are preventives against Rheumatism, Sciatica, and Gout, Chilblains, &c., and also are very beneficial in the first stages of spinal affections, &c. Although the Medical Faculty may disagree upon the true nature of Rheumatic Gout it is beyond doubt that in most cases the most effective remedy is Electricity, which is very effectually conveyed into the system by the use of these Socks worn in boots.

The ELECTRIC SOCKS produce a current acting congenially on the body, and is far superior to the prickling and disagreeable influence of an induction coil. Against spinal complaints, the first symptoms of which are numbness of the feet and pricking sensation (so called "Pins and Needles"), they act very effectively, the electric current influencing the spine through the peripheric ends of the nerves.

ELECTRIC SOCKS should be worn by those who have Rheumatic or Gouty Affections in the Feet, or are liable to coldness or chilblains in those parts. The circulation is at once stimulated, and an agreeable warmth diffused. The heat of the body induces Thermo-Electricity, the perspiration of the body evolves a galvanic current, and the Electric power is always in force.

IMPORTANCE OF WEARING ELECTRIC SOCKS.—Few are conscious of the very great advantage of wearing under the feet a medium that will not only prevent the abstraction of electricity by cold earth, but will at the same time generate in the feet those electric currents on which warmth depends.

Please forward Exact size of Feet when ordering these Socks. All Chemists keep the Electricpatent Socks.

> **CAUTION.**—Beware of the rubbishy, so-called magnetic socks that are sometimes stocked by Chemists on account of their low price—they cannot generate Electricity and are dear at any price. The Electricpatent Socks are only sold IN BOXES, price 12s. 6d. per pair. Will last for years.

Pair of Socks forwarded, post free, on receipt of Post Office Order or Cheque for 12s. 6d., to be made payable to C. B. HARNESS, Managing Director,

PALL MALL ELECTRIC ASSOC., LTD., 21, HOLBORN VIADUCT, LONDON, E.C.

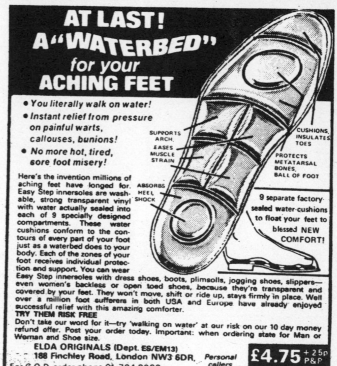

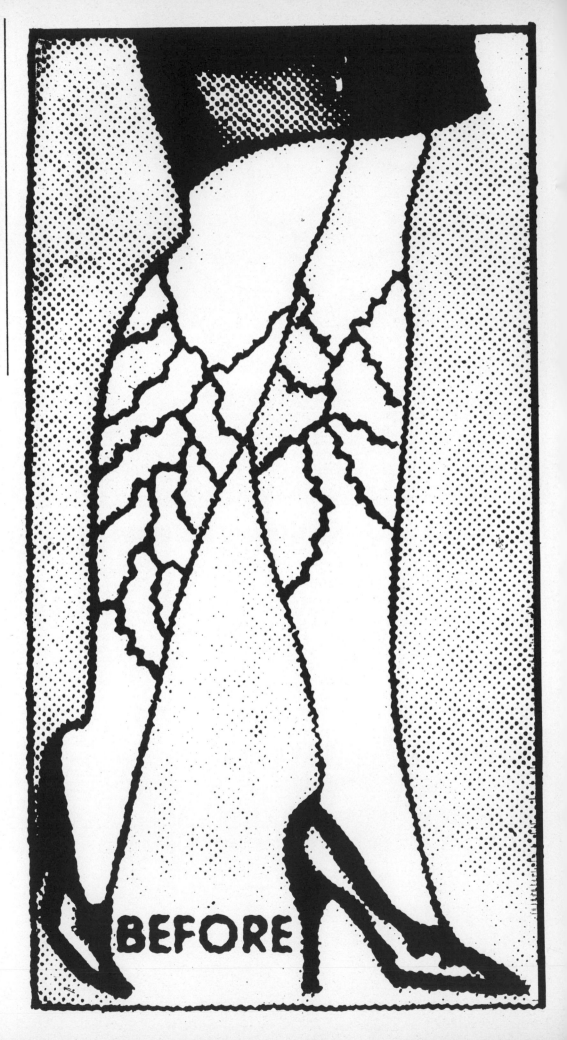

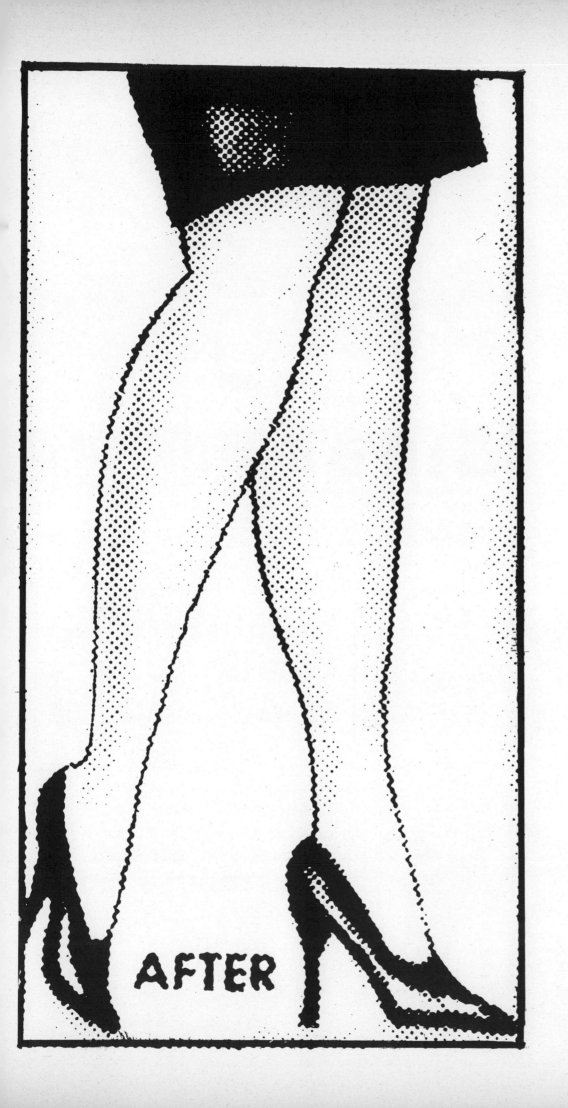

AFTER

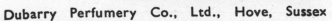

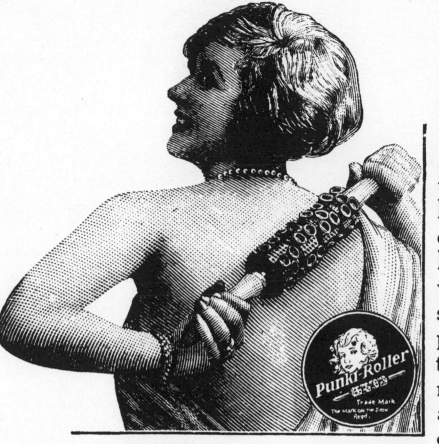

SELF-MASSAGE

AN excellent tried method of making the body supple and healthy. The 60 suction cups of the **PUNKT-ROLLER** attack the whole of the skin surface, drawing and propelling the blood through the hair-fine network of the capillary system. The use of the **Punkt-Roller** can be concentrated upon any part of the body, and, as its action is much more effective than that of Hand Massage, five to ten minutes' daily use of the **Punkt-Roller** gives much better results, while the fact that it is self-massage spares the cost of a professional masseur and makes time a matter of personal convenience.

Sluggish circulation of the blood causes bad digestion, adipose tissue, Rheumatism, Gout, Diabetes and Hardening of the Arteries; makes skin and muscles slack and ages one rapidly.

Only healthy normal circulation can free the body from impurities, uric acid and lurking germs of diseases, and absorb superfluous fat.

You can keep fit with the Punkt-Roller.

Buy a Punkt-Roller to-day. But be sure it bears the Trade Mark "Mark on the Brow." No imitations are as effective.

STANDARD MODEL 25/-
Popular Model 19/6 Face Punkt-Roller 7/6
The Punkt Friction Spray 5/-

To be obtained from all branches of

BOOTS THE CHEMISTS,

all leading General Stores in London and the Provinces, and from all first-class Chemists.

Wholesale Distributors: Punkt Products Depôt (Dept. 11), 41, Great Tower Street, London, E.C.3.

Coming Sir! THIN or **THICK** Sir?

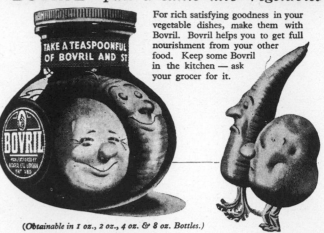
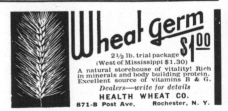

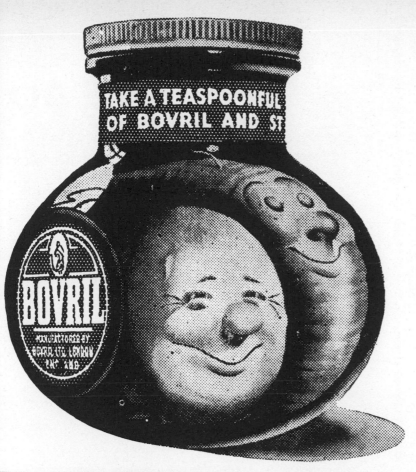

TAKE A TEASPOONFUL OF BOVRIL AND ST

BOVRIL

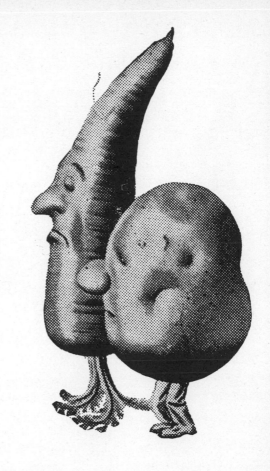

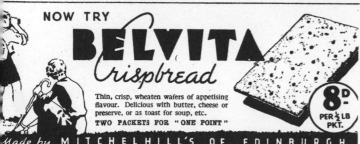

ʔOOKED FOOD

DIET

& EVERYBODY.

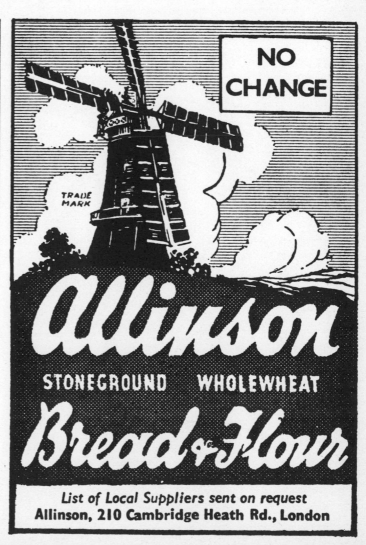

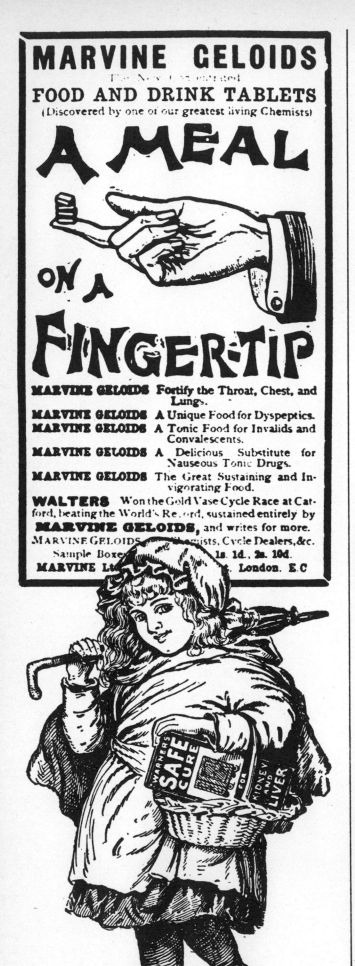

MAPLETON'S NUT FOOD CO. LTD. LIVERPOOL, 19

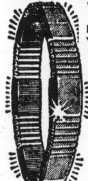

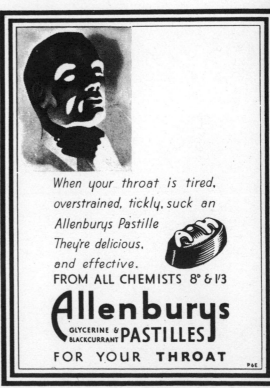

VICK BRAND VAPOUR-RUB

"ROSES" OF HEALTH

EFFERVESCENT
ANDREWS LIVER SALT
LAXATIVE

—THAT COME FROM *the* SEA

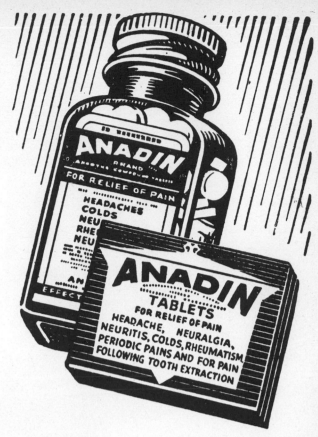

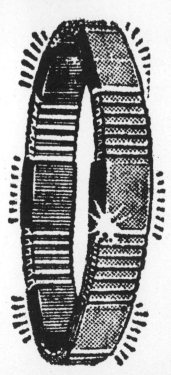

SUCHARD'S COCOA

"The cup that cheers." Sold in $\frac{1}{4}$, $\frac{1}{2}$, and 1 lb. tins.

TOBLER'S

Swiss Milk Chocolate

Hildebrand's

High Class Chocolates Pralines Fondants

Jubilee Gold Medal
London 1897

Theodor Hildebrand & Sohn

Berlin.

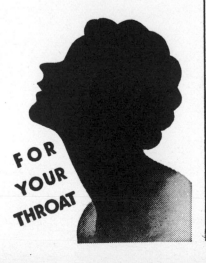

FOR YOUR THROAT

TRY ONE

GRAY DUNN & Co's RICH CREAM BISCUITS

GLASGOW

RICH CREAM BISCUITS.

UNSWEETENED
Made with
PURE CREAM.
RICH & · · · ·
· · PALATABLE.

WOODWARD'S "GRIPE WATER"

FOR ALL DISORDERS OF INFANTS & YOUNG CHILDREN

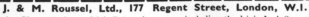

52

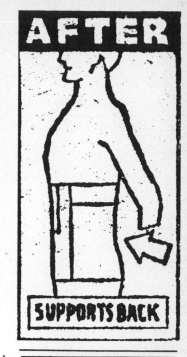

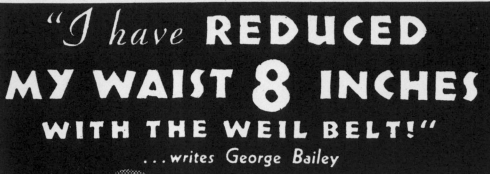

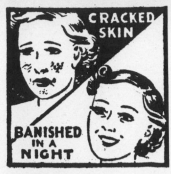

CRACKED SKIN
BANISHED IN A NIGHT

UGLY STRETCH MARKS DISAPPEAR

CHAPS
HEALED

Ugly stretch marks disappear under this (water-proof cream) In case you have forgotten there is a cream called "Markhide" that will beautify your skin even covering white patches, ugly scars left by surgery, stretch marks, pregnancy, discolorations, lines from diets. Your skin can regain its natural tone under a coating of Markhide". Markhide" comes in two shades, either one must blend with your skin or by mixing both and attaining the exact tone of your skin, you can hide any type of blemish under this cream. It will not rub off, water resistant, must be washed off with soap, water. Easy to use. Can also be used under make up
No. 160M For medium skin
No. 160R For dark skin
Try it on the money back guarantee, just send your name and address. On delivery to you, pay only $2 plus postage and C.O.D. charge, or better still just mail $2. This covers everything.

Write to: **HOWARD TRESSES —Dept. 2804A**
211 West Broadway, L.I., N.Y. 11696
FREE LATEST CATALOG OF FORMULAS FOR THE SKIN, SCALP, HAIR, FOGS JUST WRITE

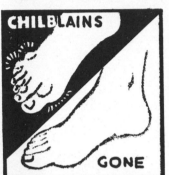

CHILBLAINS
GONE

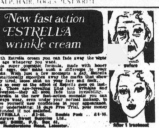

New fast action
ESTRELLA
wrinkle cream

With Estrella cream you can fade away the signs of age whenever you want. This super cosmetic formula, made with honey and eggs, can make such a difference to your looks. With just a few moments a day, Estrella transitionally smoothes away the marks that show any tired, loose skin on your face and neck. It's as easy as the effect of Estrella goes on lasting. Those age-revealing lines and wrinkles and crow's-feet—they all soon fade into invisibility. Estrella is the new fast-action cosmetic you can always wear, even under your normal makeup, to give yourself new confidence in your appearance. Our undertaking: 14 days Free Trial, your money refunded if not satisfied.
ESTRELLA £7·16. Bumble Pack £1·18. Beigrave Beauty Supplies Ltd., 63 Bedford Road, Leicester.

---

ree

Begin your season in town by giving your complexion the same care that you are bestowing upon your wardrobe. Your gown need last but a season—your complexion must be preserved for many years.

Systematic care of your skin for a few minutes each day—less time than you spend in dressing your hair—will keep your complexion in perfect condition. Provided of course that you give it the proper treatment.

MADAME HELENE

has just returned after several months of study abroad. *She will give you one treatment free of charge* to demonstrate the latest improvements in her methods which have already been so successful. Visit her studio at

381 FIFTH AVENUE
In the Alice Maynard Store

AMAMI
Henna
SHAMPOO

A delightful, powdered preparation put up in dainty envelopes with just enough Egyptian Henna to give a beautiful lustre without staining the hair. In boxes of seven packets, 60 cents.
Amami Bath Crystals will impart a delicate fragrance to your bath. Price, 75 cents, $1.50 and $3.
Try the latest Parisian Face Powder. Of pale lavender tinge. All the rage now. AMAMI SYLVIA, 50 cents a box.

Send 25c. for Bijou box containing assorted samples.

Prichard & Constance.
49 W. 23rd St., New York

Before

After 1 treatment

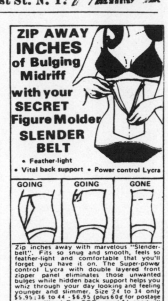

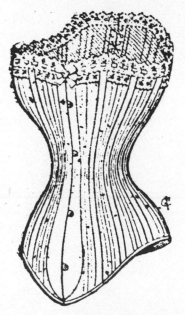

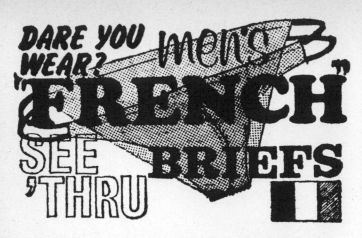

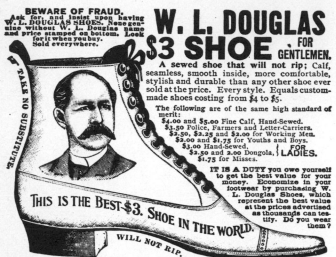

"They laughed when I sat down to play the piano"

There may have been many reasons why self-improvement was a desirable objective during the first half of this century yet the market today has lost none of its bouyancy. Although many aspects of the modern mans' adult education are now catered for by a more enlightened political and educational climate, the newspaper columns still carry a wide variety of offerings to stimulate and pamper the mind.

THE MOUTH FLUTINA

Is the latest and most charming novelty in musical instruments. It is easy to play, and makes delightful music, far excelling in quality and tone any reed instrument ever made. It is beautifully finished, resembling polished mahogany, and has silver keys, trumpets, mouth-piece and two bass keys. We guarantee this instrument to give better satisfaction than other reed instruments selling at less than $7. We are so confident of its merits and large sale, that we imported several thousand at a very low price, and propose to give the readers of the

FARM, FIELD AND FIRESIDE

the benefit of our advantage thus secured. **HOW TO GET ONE OF THESE DELIGHTFUL INSTRUMENTS FREE.** During the present year we have increased the circulation of our paper over 75,000 copies and have to-day an actual prepaid circulation larger than that of any paper published west of New York City. We still want to further increase it many thousands before January 1st, 1884, and make this **WONDERFUL OFFER:** To any one who will send us four yearly subscribe s at One Dollar each (the regular price of the paper), and twenty-five cents, to pay delivery charges, we will send one of these fine instruments free, or if you can not send subscribers we will se them for **Tw Dollars** each, and prepay all delivery charges to any place in the United States. Send money by Registered Letter, Money-Order or Express. Mention this paper. Address

FARM, FIELD AND FIRESIDE,

89 Randolph Street, Chicago, Ills.

☞ *Our readers should take advantage of this offer at once, as it will not be made again.*

BE A SUCCESSFUL ARTIST

EARN MONEY WITH PEN OR PENCIL IN SPARE TIME

Copy this sketch for free criticism.

IT is more natural for a man to draw than to read or write. But nowadays most men read and write—yet *they fear to draw.* Long before man had invented an alphabet, he drew pictures with the burnt end of a stick snatched up from his blazing cave-fire. Drawing is a *natural* way of expressing what one sees or conceives. Whether by eye-vision or mind-vision, man instinctively "pictures the thing to himself."

Send now a copy of the accompanying sketch (or a specimen of your original work), together with coupon below, and you will receive, without any charge or obligation, an *expert* and quite candid criticism of your work.

Such advice may enable you to develop a possibly hitherto unsuspected talent. That's the point—"unsuspected talent." By the JOHN HASSALL WAY your natural ability may be utilised for your own great profit, in your spare time, and in your own home.

Learning to draw by the JOHN HASSALL WAY is a fascinating pursuit which always brings pleasure and often profit.

A handsome BROCHURE containing many illustrations of the work of John Hassall, R.I., and his pupils, will be sent free. This book gives graphic details of the John Hassall Postal Course; what it is, what it has done, and what it can do for you.

The John Hassall Correspondence Art School, Dept. H 7, St. Albans.

YOU CAN LEARN TO DRAW

AT HOME—IN YOUR SPARE TIME

It's interesting and pleasant to learn the W.S.A. way. Trained Artists are capable of earning $30, $50, $75 weekly.

COMMERCIAL ART — ILLUSTRATING CARTOONING

Many of our successful graduates never studied Art before enrolling with W.S.A. YOU have the same opportunity to be an Artist. Our proven, practical training has been successful since 1914. Write today for FREE BOOK—"Art for Pleasure and Profit"—describes TWO BIG ARTISTS' OUTFITS given. State age.

Studio 1612E, WASHINGTON SCHOOL OF ART
1115-15th ST. N. W.   WASHINGTON, D. C.

BE A PASSENGER TRAFFIC INSPECTOR

OPPORTUNITIES FOR OUR TRAINED GRADUATES

Railway and Bus Lines use our trained Passenger Traffic Inspectors. Good pay to start. Advance rapidly with experience. Short home-study course prepares you and upon completion we place you at up to $135 per month, plus expenses, to start, **or refund tuition.** Interesting work; splendid opportunities. Write

STANDARD BUSINESS TRAINING INSTITUTE
Div. 2112   Buffalo, N. Y.

Law!

LEARN AT HOME

Are you adult, alert, ambitious, willing to study? Investigate LAW! We guide you step by step—furnish all texts, including 14-volume Law Library. Training prepared by leading law professors and given by members of bar. Degree of LL.B. conferred. Low cost, easy terms. Send NOW for Free, 48-page "Law Training for Leadership."

LASALLE EXTENSION UNIVERSITY, Dept. 12308-L, Chicago
A CORRESPONDENCE INSTITUTION

Wish I had $500!   MUST BE NEAR LUNCH-TIME
My Sweetheart   HATE BOSS
NEED NEW SHOES   Why Don't I Get a Raise?
GIRL WITH A RED HAT
FLORIDA   New Job

Sir Harry Lauder, Comedian.   Baroness Orczy, Author.
W. L. George, Author.   Prince Charles of Sweden.

—and others, of equal prominence, too numerous to mention here.

Pelmanism is the science of applied psychology, which has swept the world with the force of a religion. It has awakened powers in individuals, all over the world, they did not DREAM they possessed.

A remarkable book called "Scientific Mind Training" has been written about Pelmanism. IT CAN BE OBTAINED FREE. Yet thousands of people who read this announcement and who NEED this book will not send for it. "It's no use," they will say. "It will do me no good," they will tell themselves. "It's all tommyrot," others will say.

But if they use their HEADS they will realize that people cannot be HELPED by tommyrot and that there MUST be something in Pelmanism, when it has such a record behind it, and when it is endorsed by the kind of people listed here.

If you are made of the stuff that isn't content to remain a slave—if you have taken your last whipping from life—if you have a spark of INDEPENDENCE left in your soul, write for this free book. It tells you what Pelmanism is, WHAT IT HAS DONE FOR OTHERS, and what it can do for you.

The first principle of YOUR success is to do something definite in your life. You cannot afford to remain undecided, vacillating, day-dreaming, for you will soon again sink into the mire of discouragement. Let Pelmanism help you FIND YOURSELF. Mail the coupon below now—while you resolve to DO SOMETHING ABOUT YOURSELF is strong.

THE PELMAN INSTITUTE OF AMERICA

271 North Avenue   Dept. 4310   New Rochelle, N. Y.

BE A SUCCESSFUL ARTIST

EARN MONEY WITH PEN OR PENCIL IN SPARE TIME

IT is more natural for a man to draw than to read or write. But nowadays most men read and write—yet *they fear to draw.* Long before man had invented an alphabet, he drew pictures with the burnt end of a stick snatched up from his blazing

Copy this sketch for free criticism.

cave-fire. Drawing is a *natural* way of expressing what one sees or conceives. Whether by eye-vision or mind-vision, man instinctively "pictures the thing to himself."

Send now a copy of the accompanying sketch (or a specimen of your original work), together with coupon below, and you will receive, without any charge or obligation, an *expert* and quite candid criticism of your work.

Such advice may enable you to develop a possibly hitherto unsuspected talent. That's the point — "unsuspected talent." By the

He Cut off his Nose to Spite his Face.

This man is a Grammar Master of the old school. He does not believe in the "New Methods." He will not send for our **Illustrated Catalogue** of **School Aids and Material**, although if he would mention that he reads the "Ads" in the POPULAR EDUCATOR we would mail it to him without charge. Said a prominent teacher the other day: "I never dealt with any other firm as prompt and business-like in all their methods as Milton Bradley Co., Springfield, Mass., and their material is always excellent." The majority of teachers use it, and you will surely want some of it this year. Do not attempt to begin school without our Catalogue. Send 12 cents for our new Number Builder for desk-work in figures. Remember that we shall soon publish a Manual for Primary Work in Ungraded Schools.

MILTON BRADLEY CO.

Springfield, Mass.

October, 1889

"A hard man is good to find"

It's odd how sex loses its appeal when presented as coldly as the early morning catch. Yet when the imagination is allowed to roam it can be very stimulating.

An obvious observation you think, yet the principle operates even in the world of the small ad. How do 'sweet-to-eat' pants grab you? Made of pure food and in a choice of four flavours.

Or a dose of Mate herb? 'not a harmful aphrodisiac and a doctor's prescription is not required.' Yet on a different level you may find the prospect of reading the '100 dirtiest books in the world' somewhat daunting.

SECRET of ROMANCE

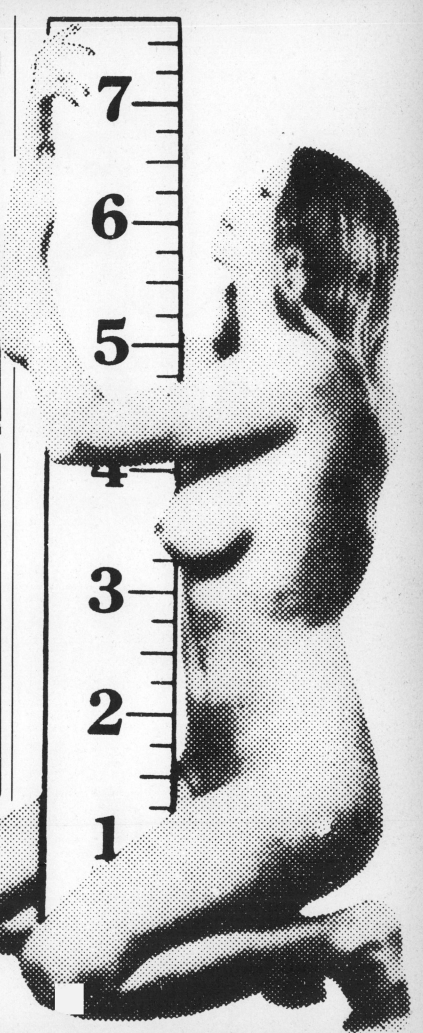

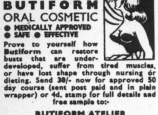

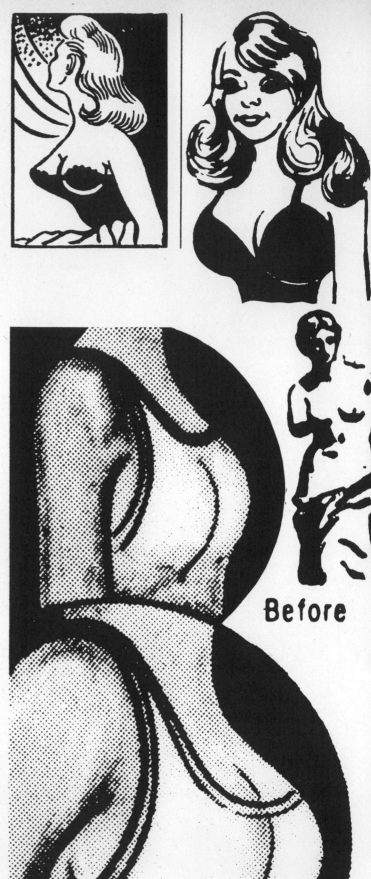

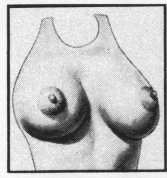
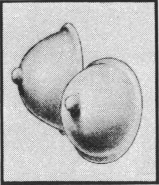
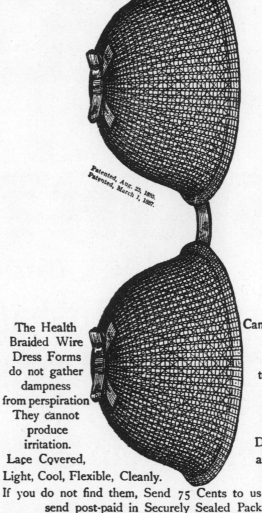

"Thank goodness, Hotpoint are going to make life easier after the war!"

When researching material for this book, it was the war years, especially those of the second world war, that made such a strong impression.

Between 1939 and 1945 the imagery of war persisted right through to the ads. It was not so much the sponsored Government advertising such as 'Careless talk costs lives,' or, in Britain—the famous 'Squanderbug,' but more the fact that the people featured in the advertisements were military personnel of one kind or another. Even the copy was sprinkled with the language of war.

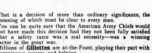

SANTA CLAUS
- a la mode !

Here I am—in war time kit—with my sack of gifts in one hand and a Stirrup Pump in the other.

Not quite the sort of Christmas I've been used to. But still it's Christmas, and still there's the same spirit of good will—even if there has to be a little less "good-cheer".

Toffee and Chocolate were my time-honoured stand-bys for Christmas. In fact, Christmas wouldn't be Christmas without them.

So I'm glad that *some* of those good things are still to be had—even although there is only half as much as usual.

Mackintosh's 'Quality Street'

★ A quarter of every Penny-a-Week contribution goes to Help Russia

WARTIME CONVERSATION PIECE

1st Housewife : Been able to get any Kellogg's lately? I'm tired of asking the grocer.

2nd Housewife : No, we haven't had Corn Flakes for some time now, but — well, you know how difficult everything is these days.

1st Housewife : I must say, I can't understand it. The Kellogg people are working day and night, working to capacity — it says so in the paper. Where *does* all the Kellogg's go to? That's what I'd like to know.

2nd Housewife : Well, for one thing, there must be hundreds of thousands more people eating Corn Flakes these days. What with bacon and eggs rationed and fish sometimes hard to get . . . After all, we've got to eat.

1st Housewife : Oh, I know *that*.

2nd Housewife : And anyway, the Kellogg Company do try to distribute all they can make as evenly as possible. It's not an easy job supplying two or three million people with breakfasts these days, you know.

1st Housewife : *Three* people — let alone *three* million — is about all *I* can manage, I must say . . . Well, I'll be getting along. Hope our turn for some more Kellogg's comes soon.

2nd Housewife : It will! And I'm sure you'll find something in the shops to tide you over till then. Goodbye.

"You've been a better club secretary since we bought you a typewriter, Jim."

Thus deliberates an early Remington portable ad. In the last decade leisure has claimed more and more of our time, whether working in the garden or taking a holiday.

The pages of the small ad. world are littered with products or services that demand a share of that time.

Perhaps 'Communicating with your plants' appeals to you. Or on a less esoteric plane 'Develop your artistic talent…and earn money with a pen or pencil.'

Or maybe even reading this book.

Comic Bald Head Rubber Mask

Change in seconds to "shiny" bald head. Look like old man. Fits over head above eyebrows, over forehead, around ears and back down to neck.

☐ 4636. Old Baldie $1.00

"THROW YOUR VOICE"

Do amazing bird and animal imitations easily. Tiny instrument fits in mouth out of sight. Learn ventriloquism; throw your voice into box, next room, under bed, make dummy talk. Fool everyone! Complete instructions with VENTRILO or DOUBLE THROAT.

30. Ventrilo Outfit. . . . 50¢

Joke Gum

Pucker Gum. Putrid.
☐ 2738. Pkg. of 5 . . 20¢
Red Hot Gum. Blazing.
☐ 2724. Pkg. of 5 . . 20¢
Garlic Gum. Awful.
☐ 2735. Pkg. of 5 . . 20¢

rough Walls!

converts to telescope

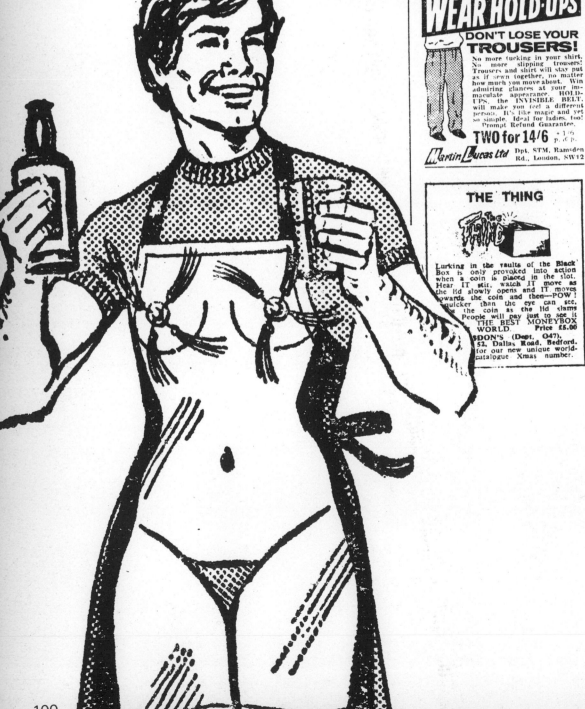

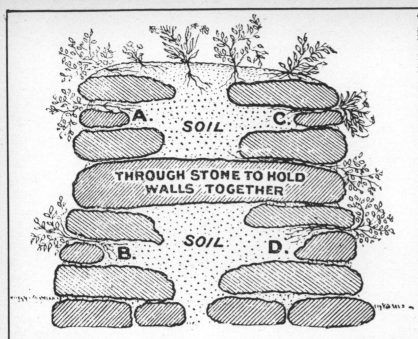

A. SOIL C.

THROUGH STONE TO HOLD WALLS TOGETHER

SOIL

B. D.

THIS SKETCH illustrates how we built a most successful **Wall Garden** in our nursery. Our **Art Catalogue** tells all about it, and gives a photo taken six months after planting. It also—by diagrams—shows how to build a rockery. It gives particulars of over **3,000** kinds of hardy plants, including **1,800** kinds of rock plants and shrubs. We've spent some 35 years in gathering together and growing hardy plants, and we now offer you our knowledge free. Can we advise **you**?

J. STORMONTH & SON, HARDY PLANT SPECIALISTS, Dept. A, **KIRKBRIDE, CARLISLE.**

OR THE STEEL FRAMED NORFOLK LEAN TO SUIT YOU BETTER? ONLY **£21·95** CARR. PAID

6' LONG 6' HIGH 3' 10" WIDE. SLIDING DOOR WILL FIT EITHER END. ROOF VENT. GLASS CLEAR FLEXIBLE PVC.

BAMBINI' ROSES

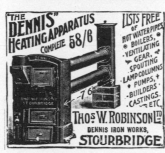
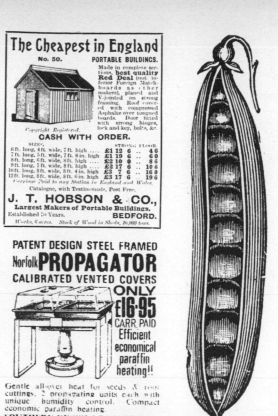

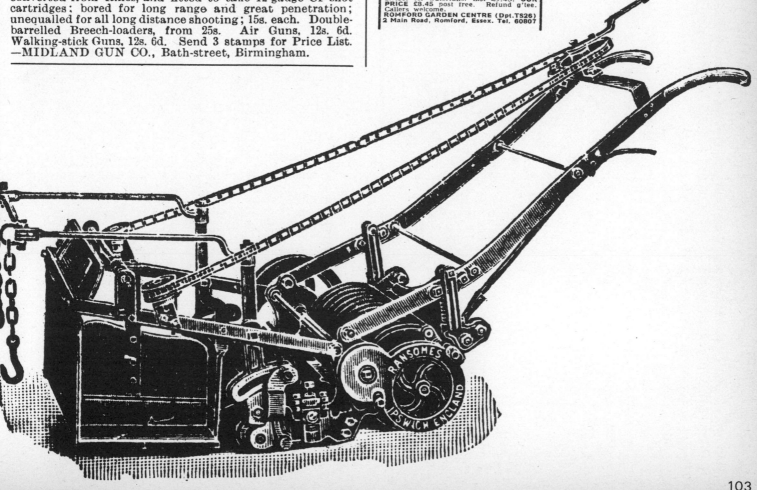

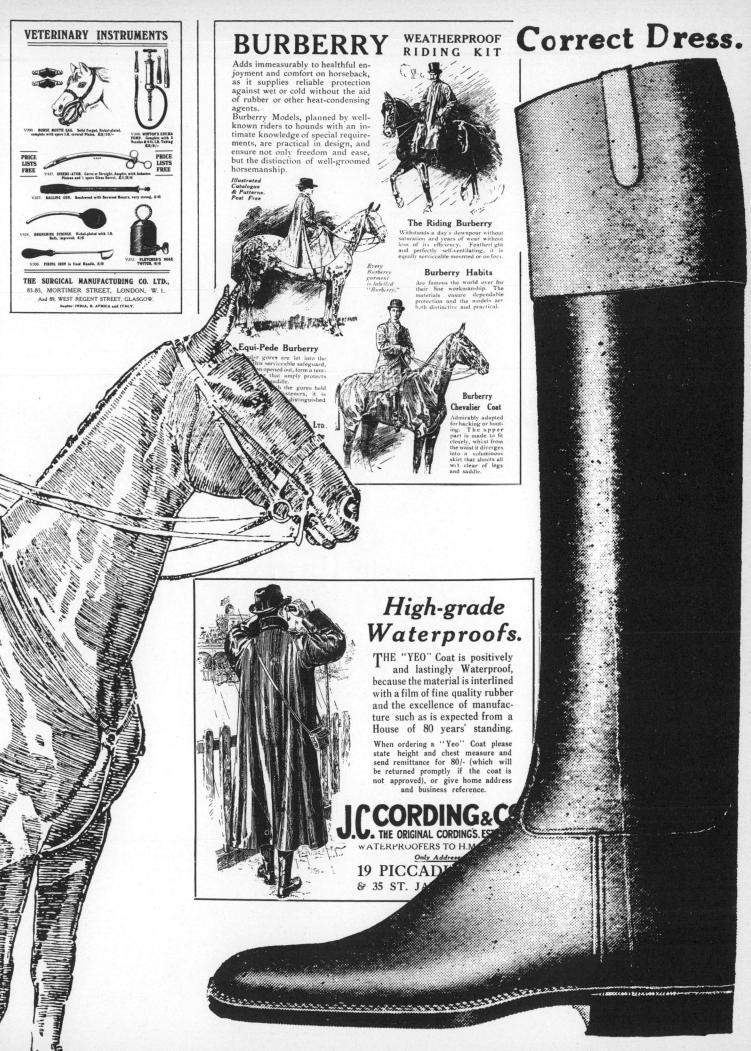
105

Past and Present . . .

Mirrors show the present, silver reflects the past; memories of a wedding-day, now many years ago; parties, when the bowl was filled with punch instead of flowers; all the years in which treasures were trusted always and only to Silvo's gentle care.

SILVO

PAROZONE YOUR LINENS AND COTTONS Snow-white loveliness assured even in these days of fuel economy. Parozone need only cold water only to achieve its brilliant result.

PAROZONE

FROM YOUR GROCER OR STORE.

Don't blame your suppliers if you cannot get all the Parozone you want. Bear with us, please . . . we are doing everything possible to maintain supplies.

To own a Creda Cooker should be the ambition of every modern housewife!

You have no idea how clean and easy cooking can be until you use a CREDA Electric Cooker.

CREDA Cookers are inexpensive, World-famous for their efficiency and incorporate all the latest labour-saving features.

Ask your Electrical Contractor or Electric Supply Authorities for full particulars, or write direct to:

The illustration shows Cat. No. C196—an ideal cooker for a family of 7 to 10.

Creda

BRITAIN'S BEST

CREDENDA CONDUITS Co., Ltd. OLDBURY, BIRMINGHAM. **ELECTRIC COOKERS**

THE DAVIS GAS STOVE CO LTD

LONDON

METROPOLITAN

Trade Mark

Gas Stoves

No. 10

Switch on ELECTRICITY

AT A TOUCH OF THE SWITCH

Add beauty & colour to your home

ELECTRIC LIGHT artistically shaded, will introduce into your home a harmony of cheerfulness and colour. Beautiful effects can be obtained with coloured lamps and an unlimited choice of modern lighting fittings, at small expense. No other form of lighting possesses such possibilities for individual taste. Your hall, your walls, table decoration, dressing table and bed lighting—all can be beautified with colourful electric light. It is not worth a little thought? One-third of your waking life is spent in artificial light. Use the best light, ELECTRIC LIGHT—cheerful and colourful.

Any electrical contractor or showroom will be pleased to assist you. Meanwhile, please write for a helpful Booklet "Light—and how to use it." It shows you how to get the most lighting beauty and convenience, how to choose the proper fittings and where to fix them. It is full of valuable information and will be sent to you post free, upon application to The British Electrical Development Association, Inc., 15, Savoy Street, Strand, London, W.C.2.

What lustre! What sheen!

The supply is restricted by the Limitations of Supplies Order, so please use sparingly. **WITH A CLOTH AND**

MIN CREAM

FOR ALL HIGHLY POLISHED SURFACES

Chiswick Products Ltd., London, W.4.

How long is a jiffy?

You will not find it in the tables of weights and measures, but every woman knows that a jiffy is the exact length of time it takes to clean and polish heavy taps with Scrubb's Ammonia. It is amazing how quickly and completely it whisks away stains and grease and dirt, leaving the metal gleaming as brightly as Uncle Henry's gold watch. Scrubb's is so helpful for scores of domestic and toilet uses that no home should ever be without a bottle.

SCRUBB'S CLOUDY AMMONIA

In bottles at 7½d. and 1/4

A HOUSEHOLD WORD FOR 100 HOUSEHOLD NEEDS

Hot Water Instantly
night or Day

EWART'S
"LIGHTNING"
GEYSER

GAS OIL OR FUEL

CATALOGUE BY
REQUEST

**346 EUSTON Rᴰ
LONDON N.W.1**

ESTABLISHED 1834

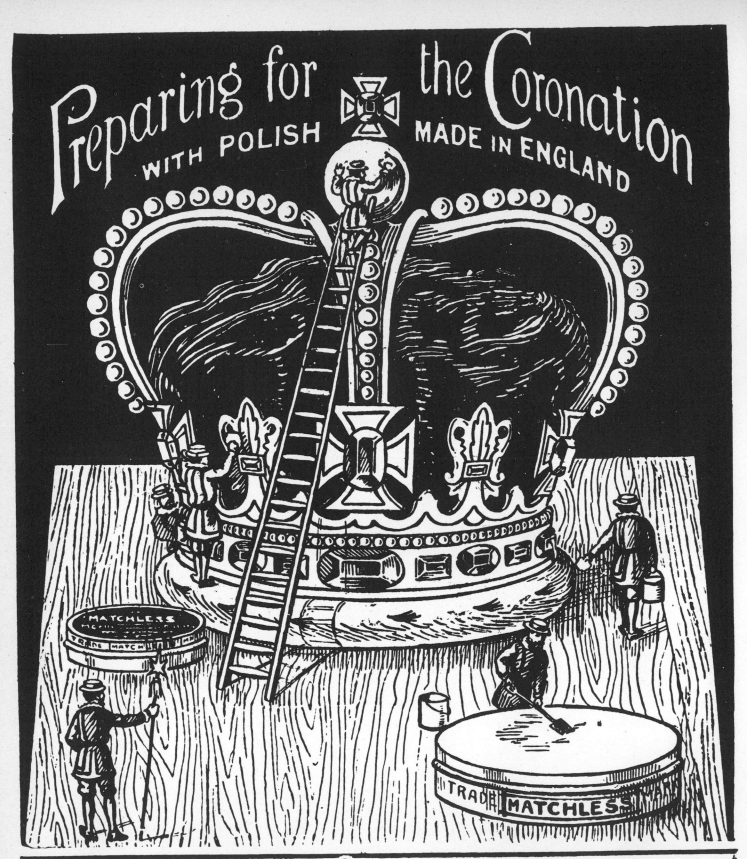

Preparing for the Coronation
WITH POLISH MADE IN ENGLAND

"Create a neighbourhood sensation..."

'......with a surplus giant weather balloon.' One lesson we have learned during the preparation of this book is that if you've got something to sell, there will always be someone to buy it, and this section is a real miscellany. 'Enhance your garden with this beautiful ornamental wishing well' quotes one ad. 'Clearance bargain. American Pool balls,' says another.

With our scepticism well and truly dented all we can say is try and avoid the rush when reading the ad. headed 'World War 2 gas masks. Just in.'

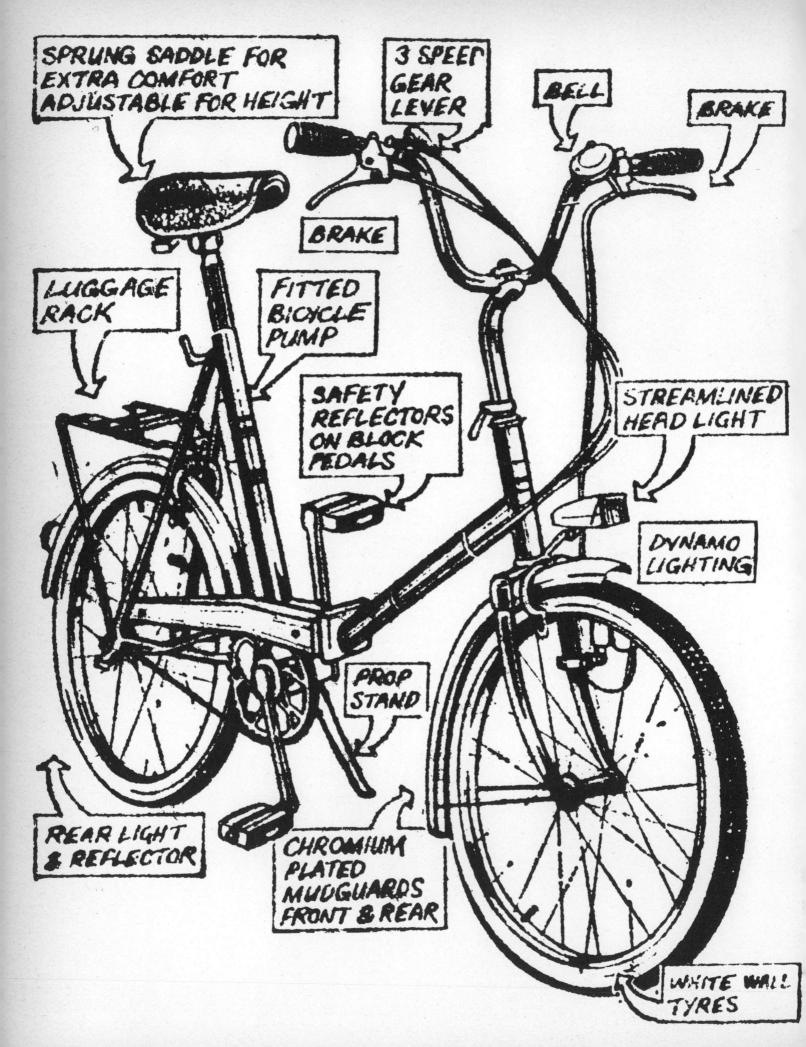

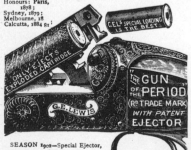
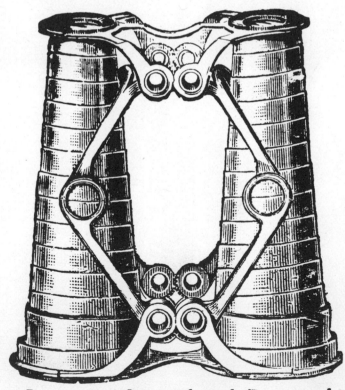

Instantly Opened and Focussed

Instantly Closed for Pocket.

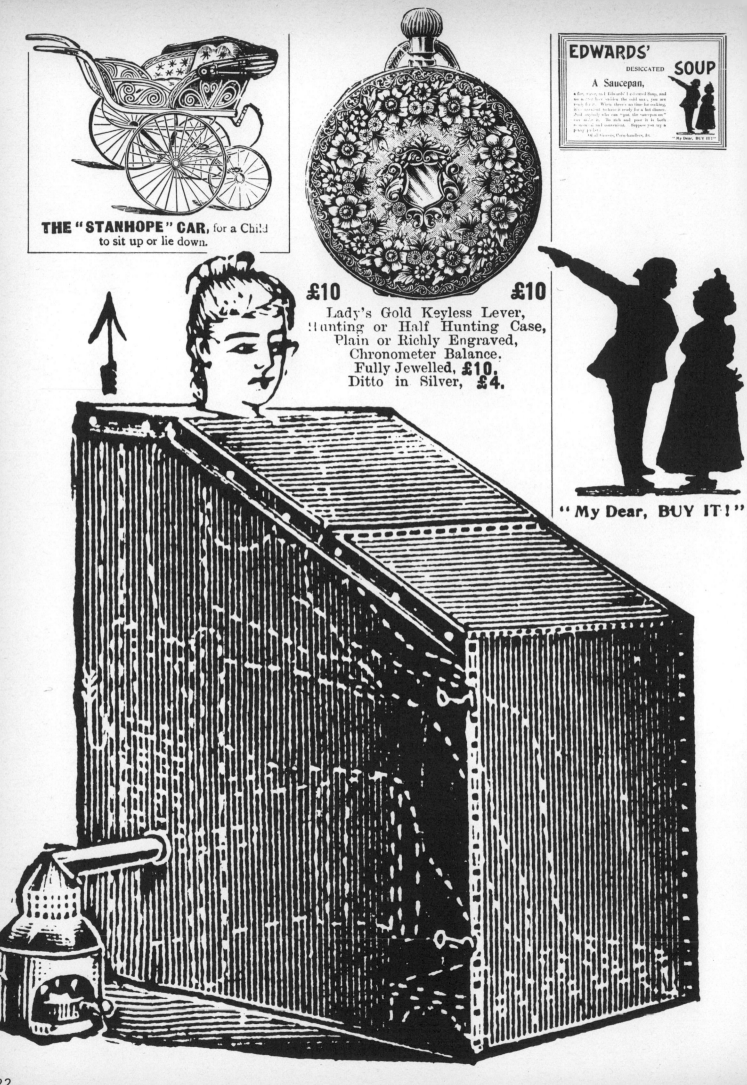

THE "STANHOPE" CAR, for a Child to sit up or lie down.

£10   £10

Lady's Gold Keyless Lever,
Hunting or Half Hunting Case,
Plain or Richly Engraved,
Chronometer Balance.
Fully Jewelled, £10.
Ditto in Silver, £4.

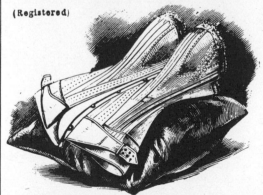
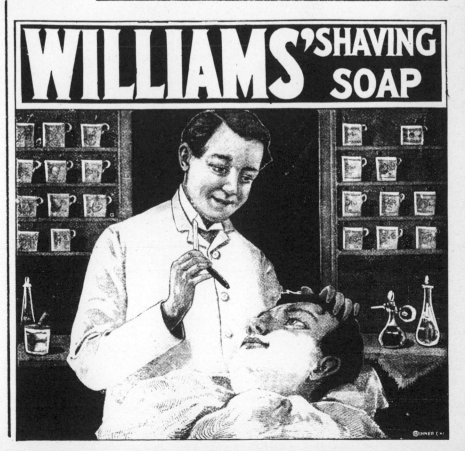

Are these your hands?

The *Salvation Army*

THE ARMY THAT SERVES ON EVERY FRONT

In innumerable overcrowded "homes" in Stepney there is no room for the growing lad; he is forced into the streets with all their perils.

What will become of him

DRIFTING

unless helpful hands come to his rescue? We hold out such hands. Numbers of youths have been, and are being, moulded into good citizens by the efforts of our workers, a large proportion of whom are honorary.

Contributions will be gratefully acknowledged by the Rev. Percy Ineson, *Superintendent,*

The East End MISSION

Central Hall, Commercial Road, Stepney, London, E.1

The Empty Chair

means a heartache to the child who has lost his Father; but it means much more. Father's advice and influence will be missing. Mother cannot look after the children whilst she is out at work. A happy home awaits fatherless and motherless boys and girls at the **ALEXANDRA ORPHANAGE,** Maitland Park, Haverstock Hill, London, N.W.3. They are trained to be useful self-reliant citizens. Will you send a gift towards the £10,000 needed each year from voluntary donations, to Fred. J. Robinson, F.C.I.S., Secretary, Alexandra Orphanage, 34-40 Ludgate Hill, London, E.C.4.